one thousand gifts
STUDY GUIDE

Also by Ann Voskamp

One Thousand Gifts (book, ebook, app, duotone edition)

One Thousand Gifts Devotional

Selections from One Thousand Gifts (giftbook)

A DARE TO LIVE FULLY

RIGHT WHERE YOU ARE

one thousand gifts

STUDY GUIDE
FIVE SESSIONS

ANN VOSKAMP
WITH SHERRY HARNEY

ZONDERVAN®
.com

ZONDERVAN.com/
AUTHORTRACKER
follow your favorite authors

ZONDERVAN

One Thousand Gifts Study Guide
Copyright © 2012 by Ann Morton Voskamp

This title is also available as a Zondervan ebook. Visit www.zondervan.com/ebooks.

Zondervan, *Grand Rapids, Michigan 49530*

ISBN 978-0-310-68438-1

Published in association with William K. Jensen Literary Agency, 119 Bampton Court, Eugene, Oregon 97404.

Cover design: Michelle Lenger
Cover photography: Masterfile®, iStockphoto®
Interior design: Beth Shagene

Printed in the United States of America

12 13 14 15 16 17 18 19 /DCI/ 20 19 18 17 16 15 14 13 12 11 10 9 8 7 6 5 4 3 2 1

contents

of note

The quotations interspersed throughout this study guide are excerpts from the book *One Thousand Gifts* by Ann Voskamp and from the video curriculum of the same name. All other resources—including the small group questions, introductions, and between-sessions materials—have been written by Sherry Harney in collaboration with Ann Voskamp.

learning to count

One, two, three, four, five, six, seven, eight, nine, and ten!

A mother sits with her little boy and counts each of his toes. She does this the day he is born. She goes through this ritual again, many times with him, in an educational routine until he learns to count all of his toes. Ten fingers and ten toes equal twenty. Eventually he learns about hundreds, thousands, and even bigger numbers like millions and billions.

Uno, dos, tres, cuatro, cinco, seis, siete, ocho, nueve, diez!

All over the world it is the same — learning to count is basic, it is core, an essential for all children and adults. As we learn to count, we discover we can keep track of things. How many dollars do we have in our bank account? How many times have we been wronged by friends and how many scars have been left on our heart? How many calories did I eat today? How many friends do we have and how many have deleted me from their friend list? We are counting people. We can't help ourselves. In English, Spanish, French, and every other language, we count and count and count.

Un, deux, trois, quatre, cinq, six, sept, huit, neuf, dix!

What do you count? What really counts in your life?

In 1897, Johnson Oatman Jr. wrote the words to a simple yet profound hymn. It was written for young people to help them learn what is really worth counting and also to remember who can be counted on. In particular, Johnson wanted people to learn that they

9

should count their blessings when times were hard. His song begins with these words:

> *When upon life's billows you are tempest tossed,*
> *When you are discouraged, thinking all is lost,*
> *Count your many blessings, name them one by one,*
> *And it will surprise you what the Lord hath done.*

Ann tells the story of her daughter, Hope, sitting down to play a hymn on the piano. She keeps the rhythm of the song, she keeps harmony, by doing nothing less than counting—that is what she does. She counts. The music teacher of a friend once said this to his students about how to keep the right beat of a song: "When you are a musician and you stop counting, it's like running around in the forest, in the dark, without a flashlight."

When you are believer and you stop counting blessings, it's like running around in the forest, on the edge of a cliff, in the dark, without a flashlight.

Without counting, the song loses harmony.

And without counting blessings, our lives lose the song, the light—the beat of God's heart.

There is hope and transformative power in counting our blessings and naming the good gifts of God—because we encounter the power of God Himself in our lives. If you want to discover the rhythms of grace, joy, and true thankfulness, count the gifts God has given and the ones He is giving you even at this moment.

Write them down, express them in words, notice them, and celebrate each one. Start with ten, then take off your shoes and count ten more gifts. Now you have twenty. Keep going: a hundred gifts, two hundred, and you will discover there are even more. When you get to a thousand gifts, you will be getting warmed up.

How long will it take to list all the gifts God has given you? Let's start together and continue counting for the rest of our lives ... and forever. Who wants to miss the beat of His heart?

One gift, two gifts, three gifts ...

SESSION 1

attitude of gratitude

Introduction

Picture a timeline. It is filled with years, months, days, hours, and countless seconds. On a timeline every moment looks the same. If you could pluck off one minute it would look just like every other minute. A simple span of sixty seconds. It seems like nothing special. It appears to be nothing unique.

Yet, all of us have minutes in our lives that shape us. Something happens in that sixty-second blip on the timeline that is deeply and profoundly personal. It was not just another minute in the history of the world.

As you look back on the timeline of your life, many of the days and weeks blur together, but there are minutes that will stand out for the rest of your life. Seared in your memory are the sounds, feelings, images, and even the smells of those moments.

None of us live long on this earth without recording one of those unforgettable experiences. Not one of us can travel the rugged roads of earth and avoid all of the painful potholes. It does not matter where you live, how much money you have, how much you love God, how careful you might be, how much faith you exercise, or how persistently you pray. Hurt and heartache are truly unavoidable.

In a moment, without even seeing it coming, we all hit life's unexpected potholes and feel jarring pain. The question is not: *Will you and I have these moments of loss and dizzying confusion?* The real issue is: *How will we respond to these inevitable and unavoidable moments?* When we discover the secret to a heart of gratitude, we can face these certain moments with grace, strength, and even what seems impossible: joy.

"There's a reason I am not writing the story and God is. He knows how it all works out, where it all leads, what it all means . . . I don't."

Talk About It

When you look back on the timeline of your story, tell about a moment you hit a pothole in your journey of life.

Video Notes

As you watch the video for session one, use the following outline to record anything that stands out to you.

Wounded moments that close our hands

Grace

Eucharisteo: grace, thanksgiving, and joy

Thanksgiving precedes the miracle

Eyes on God, open hands in thanks

The list of one thousand gifts

At all times, thank God

"*The* gift list is thinking upon His goodness —
and this, this pleases Him most!"

Video Discussion and Bible Study

1. Tell about a moment in your life that was hard and painful and
   looked nothing like a gift, until later you began to discover that a
   gift was wrapped up in the pain of that moment.

2. What are some of the things that can cause us to close our hands
   and hearts to God?

   What specifically has helped you keep your hands and heart open,
   even through hard times?

"*Living* with losses, I may choose to still say yes. Choose to say yes to what He freely gives. Could I live that—the choice to open the hands to freely receive whatever God gives? If I don't, I am still making a choice ... the choice not to."

3. Ann observes that there is a distinct difference between *receiving* the grace God offers at the cross of Jesus and *being filled* with grace to the point of overflowing ... every day. If a person has received the grace of Jesus and also walks in the fullness of that grace to the point of overflowing, what might this grace-extending life look like at *one* of these moments:

   • When an opportunity to serve a person in need presents itself
   • When someone betrays and hurts us deeply
   • When we get unexpected hard news
   • When a family member is unkind or insensitive
   • When the future is uncertain and we feel anxious or fearful

"*Thanksgiving* is the evidence of our acceptance of whatever He gives. Thanksgiving is the manifestation of our Yes! to His grace."

4. **Read:** Matthew 26:26–29 and 1 Corinthians 11:23–26. When Jesus broke the bread and offered the cup, He spoke this beautiful word: *eucharisteo*. This one word captures three distinct and powerful ideas. How did Jesus reveal each of the following in His institution of the Lord's Supper (the Eucharist)?

Grace

Thanks

Joy

What can we do to deepen and expand our thankfulness, joy, and experience of grace?

5. **Read:** John 11:38–44. Ann talks about thanksgiving raising the dead. What are some connections between thanksgiving and new life being unleashed in the dark and dead places of life?

6. In the video, Ann says, "Jesus offers thanksgiving for even that which will break Him and crush Him and wound Him." How could Jesus express thanksgiving even as He faced the cross? How can Jesus' example shape your own response to times of pain and loss?

"Thanksgiving—giving thanks in everything—prepares the way that God might show us His fullest salvation in Christ."

7. **Read:** 2 Chronicles 20:12–22. How was thankfulness connected to the victory God's people experienced in this passage? How does a thankful spirit lead to victory in our lives today?

8. Why is it so hard to express *eucharisteo* thankfulness when we are going through a time of pain, struggle, and darkness? What can help us remain truly thankful in these seasons of life?

"As long as thanks is possible, then joy is always possible. Whenever, meaning—now; wherever, meaning—here."

9. Take a minute to list five gifts you already have—anything that reveals God's grace, makes you thankful, and unleashes joy in your life—and then share one item from your list with the rest of the group.

-

-

-

-

-

How does a life filled with *eucharisteo* profit us as well as bring delight to the heart of God?

"We only enter the full life if our faith gives thanks."

Closing Prayer

Take time as a group to pray in any of the following directions:

- Thank God for the good gifts He has given you.
- Invite God to teach you how to experience *eucharisteo* in the hard times of life.
- Confess where you have forgotten to be thankful for God's unmerited gifts.
- Ask Jesus to so fill you with His joy and grace that others see it and are drawn near to Him.
- Pray for your family members and friends to discover the truth that grace, thanksgiving, and joy can be theirs through an intimate and living relationship with Jesus.

"Prayer without ceasing is only possible in a life of continual thanks."

between sessions

My Gifts

Read: Philippians 4:11–12. Ann articulates that the secret to living joyfully in every situation is something that is learned. She shares that "practice is the hardest part of learning, and training is the essence of transformation."

After each small group gathering, you will have a space like the one that follows to stretch yourself, practice *eucharisteo*, and make a fresh new list of gifts God has given you. (Or consider starting your own separate gratitude journal.) Be creative, think deep, and reflect on big things as well as very small ones. You don't have to be poetic or a great writer, just honest.

Start by listing up to twenty gifts of God's grace.

-
-
-
-
-
-
-
-

-
-
-
-
-
-
-
-
-
-

Look for opportunities to share some of the gifts on your list with others in the coming week. And ask them what gifts God has placed in their lives.

"The brave who focus on all things good and all things beautiful and all things true, even in the small, who give thanks for it and discover joy even in the here and now, they are the change agents who bring fullest Light to all the world."

My Timeline

In the space provided on the following pages, create personal timelines for up to three moments of loss, pain, and struggle in your life. Note how each situation impacted your past and has influenced your present.

Moment 1

When I was _____ years old
  I experienced:

This moment impacted my life in some of the following ways:

  •

  •

  •

  •

This moment influences my life today in the following ways:

  •

  •

  •

  •

Moment 2

When I was _____ years old
   I experienced:

This moment impacted my life in some of the following ways:

-

-

-

-

This moment influences my life today in the following ways:

-

-

-

-

Moment 3

When I was _____ years old

I experienced:

This moment impacted my life in some of the following ways:

-

-

-

-

This moment influences my life today in the following ways:

-

-

-

-

"When we lay the soil of our hard lives open to the rain of grace
and let joy penetrate our cracked and dry places, let joy soak
into our broken skin and deep crevices, life grows."

Eucharisteo Mentors

By God's hand and kindness, we all know people who have revealed lives of *eucharisteo* grace, thanksgiving, and joy.

Reflect on your journey of faith by listing a few people—past or present—who have been models and mentors when it comes to living like Jesus.

-
-
-
-
-

Next, pause to thank God for the examples these people have shown you and reflect on how you can internalize their example and let it continue to shape your faith and life.

Finally, during the next week, send an email or a handwritten thank-you note to one or two of these people. Let them know some of the ways you have seen their example of walking in grace, thanksgiving, and joy. Thank them for walking closely with God and being an example of *eucharisteo*.

Journal

Use the space provided to reflect on any of the following topics:

- How you are doing when it comes to experiencing grace in your life.
- How you are doing when it comes to expressing thankfulness to God and to others.
- How you might grow in your expressions of thankfulness and joy.
- What steps you might take to live a life filled with a spirit of *eucharisteo*.

Recommended Reading

As you reflect on what you have learned in this session, you may want to read the opening section of the book, *One Thousand Gifts* by Ann Voskamp, chapters 1–3. In preparation for session two, you might want to read chapters 4–5.

grace in the moment

Introduction

In Hawaii there are glass-bottom boats that take tourists for rides across the beautiful blue Pacific waters. People reserve expensive seats to pack onto one of these crowded vessels and get a chance to see what lies just below the surface of the ocean — colorful fish, intricate coral, and maybe even an occasional giant sea turtle.

As the boat captain accelerates to leave the harbor and head to a sightseeing destination, those on the boat wander away from the clear glass-bottom viewing area. They do this because there is nothing to see. Everything below them becomes a blur, lost in the darkness of the waters beneath. The faster the boat goes, the less there is to see.

Finally, the captain pulls into a cove or along a reef and brings the boat to a stop. When everything is still and the boat is no longer moving, the scene below comes into focus: a world of beauty, graceful motion, color, and otherworldly shapes. All of it is just feet away, but would never be visible if the boat kept moving along at a rapid pace. The only way to drink in the underwater magnificence is to slow down and come to a stop.

A ride on one of these boats creates a picture of our lives. How often do we skim along the surface of life, accelerating and covering great distances, but never stopping to appreciate the beauty God has placed before us? When we slow, stop, notice, reflect, and give thanks — it's right there: the goodness and grace of God all around us.

"Giving thanks for one thousand things is ultimately an invitation to slow time down with the weight of full attention."

Talk About It

Name some of the things that are causing you to rush headlong through life.

"*In our rushing, bulls in china shops, we break our own lives.*"

Video Notes

As you watch the video for session two, use the following outline to record anything that stands out to you.

The danger of a hurried life

God's invitation ... slow down and live fully in the moment

Thanksgiving makes time

The hard *eucharisteo*

The habit of keeping a gratitude journal

What if the things that feel like trouble are gifts of grace?

All new life comes from dark places—even resurrection follows a cross and dark tomb

Slowing down to see, to surrender, to savor the goodness of God

"*Don't I always have the choice to be fully attentive? Simplicity is ultimately a matter of focus.*"

Video Discussion and Bible Study

1. Describe a time or season of your life when you were moving so rapidly that you skimmed over many of the good gifts God has given you. As you look back, what did you miss because of the sheer speed you were moving? How did thankfulness flee as well?

   How do you feel about that season now? How might this recollection inform the next season when hurry seems to set the pace?

"Hurry always empties a soul."

2. **Read:** Exodus 3:1–6, 11–15 and John 8:48–59. God used a specific name for Himself in His conversation with Moses. Centuries later, Jesus used this same name for Himself (much to the dismay of the religious leaders of His day). What is this name and what does it teach us about the God we worship?

"When I'm present, I meet I AM, the very presence of a present God. In His embrace, time loses all sense of speed and stress and space and stands so still and … holy. Here is the only place I can love Him."

3. **Read:** John 1:1–14. What does this passage in John's gospel teach us about how God entered time and space? How did Jesus come, and why did He step out of eternity into our time and space?

4. In the video, Ann asks this question: "Why is *eucharisteo* the answer to the time starved and soul famished?" How would you answer Ann's question?

What are some of the daily miracles we might miss or skim over if we aren't intentional to be thankful in the blur of each day?

"*Eucharisteo always precedes a miracle.*"

5. **Read:** Psalm 46:10–11, Psalm 127:1–2, and Genesis 2:1–3. What does God have to say about slowing down, resting, and finding quiet in our lives? How do you read this thread throughout the Bible?

How is God Himself an example of slowing down and finding rest?

6. If you have developed some skills or abilities to slow down and drink deeply of the good things we can discover with a sensible pace of life, share what you have learned with your group. How can the examples of other group members living a slower pace of life help and inspire us?

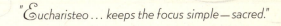

"*Eucharisteo … keeps the focus simple — sacred.*"

7. In the video, Ann tells the story of her son Levi's accident and the struggle that ensued. Sometimes, in the dark, hard, and painful times of life, grace shines through. In these moments we sense God's presence and taste grace in fresh new ways. Tell of such a breakthrough of God's presence into one of your dark moments.

How did thankfulness eventually become part of this experience in your life?

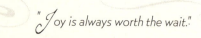

"*Who* would ever know the greater graces of comfort and perseverance, mercy and forgiveness, patience and courage, if no shadows fell over a life?"

8. In some of life's moments, a joy-filled and thankful spirit can seem far away, elusive, or even improper. How can we practice *eucharisteo* in such situations?

"*Joy* is always worth the wait."

9. How does an active and authentic prayer life help increase our thankfulness? Conversely, how can a lack of prayer become a roadblock to thankfulness?

10. What is one way you can slow down in the coming week? What step or steps will you take to make room for quiet, reflection, grace, and thankfulness?

What tends to keep you from slowing down and how can your group members pray for you and encourage you in your effort to do so?

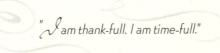

"*I am thank-full. I am time-full.*"

Closing Prayer

Spend time in your group praying in any of the following directions:

- Thank God that He is patient with you, even when you rush around and hurry after things that don't satisfy your soul.
- Pray for eyes to see where you are rushing and how you can slow down.
- Ask for strength to meet God and experience thankfulness even in the dark and painful times of uncertainty.
- Invite the Holy Spirit to grow your ability to notice the good gifts around you and slow down to appreciate them.
- Pray for strength to meet God in the hard times and be a person of *eucharisteo* even when it is a challenge.

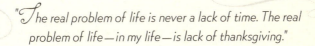

"*The real problem of life is never a lack of time. The real problem of life—in my life—is lack of thanksgiving.*"

Many Places to Gather Gifts

We never know when God will surprise us with a good gift. At any moment we could slow down and notice a gift He has gently placed in our lap. Set up a number of different places you can gather your list of good gifts. It could be a dry-erase board on your refrigerator, a journal in your purse, a list app on your smartphone, an index card in your wallet, a note pad in your glove box, a folder in your school bag, a document on an iPad, a file in your computer, or somewhere else. Make sure at least one of your lists is in a place others will see it so that they can be inspired to begin their own lists.

"To receive a gift the knees must bend humble and the hand must lie vulnerably open and the will must bow to accept whatever the Giver chooses to give."

My Gifts

Use the space below to list ten gifts of grace, or continue to use your own journal.

-
-
-
-
-

-
-
-
-
-

Stacking Stones

The people of Israel had a tradition of stacking stones as a memorial to remind them of something great that God had done. Cross the Jordan ... stack some stones. God delivers us from our enemies ... pile up some stones. Then, when children and grandchildren saw a stack of stones and asked, "Mama, what does that stack of stones mean?" she could tell the story of God's faithfulness again. When a child asked, "Dad, there is another stack of stones; can you tell me the story that goes with the stack?" Dad could recite the history of God's work among His people.

When we get moving too fast, we no longer collect memories, stack stones, or write journals. We don't have time to gather our thousand gifts and revel in God's goodness. *We no longer tell the stories of God.*

Take time to identify three or four ways you could stack stones, remember, and have occasions to tell stories of God's goodness in your life, family, and journey of faith. This can happen in many shapes and forms: scrapbooks, a collective family journal left out on a side table to doodle in and record memories, a slide show of a family vacation on a computer screen, a wall covered in easel paper to invite the writing down of God's goodness, notches marking the progressing heights of children on a door frame, family traditions of storytelling, a journal entry, pictures on a wall, a blog post, one photo a day with your camera or phone, and so on.

It's absolutely never too late to begin to stack up all of God's goodnesses. Pick one of these ideas and do (or begin doing) it in the coming week. Let this be a first step in slowing down and stacking stones.

Journal

Use the space provided to reflect on any of the following topics:

- When do I naturally slow down? How can I build on these life patterns?
- What makes it hard for me to slow down and drink in God's grace? Fear? Sadness? Pride? Woundedness? Sin? What can I do to overcome these things?
- How can I discover God as the "I AM" who is with me at all times and in all places?
- What are some of the memorials and stacks of stones my parents and grandparents set up and what can I learn from them?
- What are dark places I am walking through right now and how can I anticipate God bringing me into the light, with time?

Recommended Reading

As you reflect on what you have learned in this session, you may want to reread chapters 4–5 of the book, *One Thousand Gifts* by Ann Voskamp. In preparation for session three, you might want to read chapters 6–7.

SESSION 3

all is grace

Introduction

Her dad had wanted a boy.

After watching the birth of three girls in a row, her dad had prayed that the fourth would be a boy. When girl number four emerged into the air of this world, her father smiled.

And decided it was time to pass on his name. Daughter number four was named after him—"Johnny."

She was an active kid. She loved horses. She swam. She climbed trees. In her late teens, Johnny—now going by "Joni"—dove into the Chesapeake Bay and her life changed forever. A warm and beautiful day went dark and cold when Joni hit the bottom of the bay with the top of her head and immediately became a quadriplegic.

For the next two years Joni battled through rehabilitation, faced the depths of depression, considered suicide, and questioned her faith. It was an ugly time, a season of brokenness on many levels, a time of struggle. And—strangely—the birth of indescribable beauty.

Over the next four decades, Joni Eareckson Tada would learn to paint by holding a brush in her teeth and produce stunning works of art. She would write award-winning books, record music albums, get married, star in a movie, and become a powerful advocate for those with special needs. She would be used of Christ to be His indescribable beauty and draw countless broken lives to wholeness in Him.

Today, Joni leads a ministry called Joni and Friends and continues to write, speak, and minister for her Lord around the world.

The most ugly and painful moment of Joni's life? God used it to be the very catalyst for a life filled with beauty and service in the name of Jesus.

This is the way of God, His way that He calls His people to wildly trust—sometimes what looks ugly at first glance is the birthplace of God's most exquisite gifts.

"The secret to joy is to keep seeking God where we doubt He is."

Talk About It

As you look back at your own life, linger in the difficult places: how has God taken up thin, papery ashes and turned even black ugliness into something of beauty?

Video Notes

As you watch the video for session three, use the following outline to record anything that stands out to you.

The ugly-beautiful

Sunflowers and flying toast

Seeing God's face in the messes of life

Looking heavenward ... a first step toward *eucharisteo*

Thanksgiving precedes the miracle

One grace after another

Wrestling, soft hearts, tears, and grace

All is grace

"The truly saved have eyes of faith and lips of thanks."

Video Discussion and Bible Study

1. Ann tells the story of her two boys sitting at the kitchen table going to war with stares, words, and toast. In the midst of the tension, pain, and struggle, she longs to see the face of Jesus and experience *eucharisteo*, but it is hard to find. Tell about a time you felt surrounded by situations out of your control and that God was hard to find.

"The discipline of thanks only comes with practice."

2. **Read:** Luke 9:28–36. Peter, James, and John went with Jesus up on the mountain … into a place of holy air and God-encounter. God was present and two great heroes of faith showed up: Moses and Elijah. The three disciples wanted to set up camp and stay.

   What are some of the spiritual mountaintop experiences you have enjoyed? What is it about these times that make us want to linger? How have you then entered back into the plains and valleys of ordinary life?

"Behold glory and be held by God."

3. Shortly after Jesus, Peter, James, and John descended the Mount of Transfiguration, they encountered a demon-possessed boy and his distraught father (Luke 9:37–43). The pain of real life came crashing down.

   What are some of the daily challenges, struggles, and pains you face as you walk through a normal week in the valley of life?

   How can we pray for grace and eyes to see Jesus right in the middle of conflict and pain? Why can this kind of prayer be so difficult?

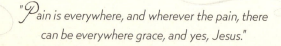

"Pain is everywhere, and wherever the pain, there can be everywhere grace, and yes, Jesus."

4. How did Jesus see good and beauty in situations where everyone else saw only a mess? Can you think of a story from the life of Jesus that is an example of this?

How does looking at the ugly and hard situations of life through the lens of Jesus change the way we see?

5. **Read:** Matthew 14:15–21. When Jesus turned His gaze and heart upward, He gave thanks. This *eucharisteo* moment in the life of Jesus models something transformative for us. Tell about a time when you turned your eyes upward and God transformed your attitude, outlook, and circumstances.

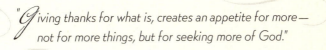

"*Giving thanks for what is, creates an appetite for more —
not for more things, but for seeking more of God.*"

6. In the video, Ann says, "Thanksgiving always precedes the miracle." How have you experienced this to be true? Not necessarily because of what you experienced, but how you encountered God?

What stands in the way of thankfulness when times are hard? What can help us enter into thanks even when things seem dark and ugly around us?

7. **Read:** Genesis 32:22–32. Ann sat at the table with an angry and hurting boy and told this simple story of a man wrestling through the night and meeting with God. How was Jacob's life transformed through this God-encounter? How were the dark and the pain connected to the way God transformed him?

Tell about a time you encountered God and found yourself changed.

8. All is grace! Is it? Are there things in your life that you still can't count as graces from God? How can you trust our God—that nothing is beyond the reach of His redemption? How can your group members pray for you as you seek to find beauty in the ugly places of your life and past?

9. Describe an ugly and painful experience that you were sure would never become a source of grace, but for which you now can actually express *eucharisteo* thanks.

10. How can you use what you know of God's faithfulness in the past to help you trust Him in the future?

"*Eucharisteo* opens the eyes wider, the heart deeper."

Closing Prayer

Spend time in your group praying in any of the following directions:

- Thank God that He is the One who can truly help us find beauty in that which seems only ugly in the world's eyes.
- Give God praise for the calm, beautiful, and peace-filled mountaintop experiences He has blessed you with.
- Pray for courage to walk back into the valley where demons live, gazes are like daggers, and hard-edged toast can fly in our faces.
- Ask the Spirit to help you stay committed and focused to find treasure under the grit and grime of this life.
- Invite God to help you notice that He is near. Pray for grace when you miss His presence and later have to say, "God was right here and I did not even notice."
- Pray for strength to wrestle well and hold on to God with all your might.

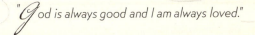

"*God* is always good and I am always loved."

My Gifts

Use the space below or your own journal to list ten more gifts of grace.

-
-
-
-
-
-
-
-
-
-

Treasure Hunt

Many of us went on treasure hunts as children. Someone would make a treasure map where "X" marked the spot and off we would go searching. As adults, we give up on these childish ways.

Maybe it is time to begin again. Elizabeth Browning and Ann Voskamp seem to think there is buried treasure in the ordinary moments of life, even in the seemingly dark, ugly, and painful moments.

It can be easy to add to your list of a thousand gifts when the sun is shining and all is well with your soul. However, during the coming week, the goal is to seek out treasure under the piles of dirt or deep in the sea of confusion. Make it a challenge, a treasure hunt—a searching for God. Joy is to find God where one doubts He can be found.

Look at the hard, painful, and conflict-filled moments. You might have to dig. You will definitely have to pray, "Lord, help me see Your face." You may have to look even more closely, dig even deeper, and then pray some more. But if you persist, you will see it ... treasure. *Christ.* Beauty in the ugly of life.

Write down where you looked and dug and what treasure you found. How you found more of Christ Himself. Come up with three buried treasures if you can.

1. The hard place I dug and searched:

    The treasure and gift I discovered:

2. The hard place I dug and searched:

    The treasure and gift I discovered:

3. The hard place I dug and searched:

The treasure and gift I discovered:

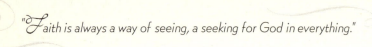

"Faith is always a way of seeing, a seeking for God in everything."

Practicing God's Presence

Ann suggests that we don't have to always change what we see, but we can adjust how we see things.

Note two or three perplexing situations in your life and then write down, with stark honesty, how you see them.

1. My situation, struggle, or ugly place:

When I'm honest, this is how I see this situation:

2. My situation, struggle, or ugly place:

When I'm honest, this is how I see this situation:

3. My situation, struggle, or ugly place:

When I'm honest, this is how I see this situation:

Now, revisit each situation and consider a couple of new ways you could look at it. How might you adjust your perspective or the way you see what is happening in your life or the life of someone you love?

1. A new way of seeing this situation:

   •

   •

   •

2. A new way of seeing this situation:

   •

   •

   •

3. A new way of seeing this situation:

   •

   •

   •

The next time you walk into this same old situation, seek to come with new eyes. Adopt the new perspective you wrote about above. Turn your eyes up and look into the face of God. Let your new eyes allow you to see God and grace ... the beauty of Christ.

Journal

Use the space provided to reflect on any of the following topics:

- My ugly-beautiful moments.
- My ugly moments, experiences, and situations in which I still have not been able to see the beauty God has hidden below the surface.
- My holy mess moments when things seem to be spiraling down, but I know God is still near.
- Prayers for dear friends who feel trapped in the painful and ugly places of life and can't seem to find God's treasures or see His face … yet.

Recommended Reading

As you reflect on what you have learned in this session, you may want to reread chapters 6–7 of the book, *One Thousand Gifts* by Ann Voskamp. In preparation for session four, you might want to read chapters 8–9.

trust: the bridge to joy

Introduction

When it was designed, it was destined to become the longest suspension bridge in the world. John Roebling engineered the Brooklyn Bridge in New York, and its two towers became the tallest structures in the Western Hemisphere at that time in history.

Tragically, Roebling was injured less than a month before the groundbreaking of the mammoth project and died. His son, Washington, was also an engineer and he took up where his father left off. Washington fell ill in 1872 and lost his ability to walk and write, and his vision was severely impaired. Not even this stopped Washington Roebling or his wife.

Emily Roebling learned engineering and stepped in as her husband Washington's representative while he watched from a distance with binoculars and gave instructions, as he was able. When the bridge was completed, Emily was celebrated as the first person to ride across this amazing structure.

Most of us have driven across bridges of all sizes and sorts and rarely take note of their structure, complexity, and what it must have taken to build them. We have no idea of the effort, toil, and sacrifice people have invested to help us cross over with ease.

Bridges take us safely from one shore to another. They carry us over an expanse we could not cover without their help. As we journey through this life, at times we need a bridge over the fears, pains, losses, and craziness swirling treacherously around us. God does not promise to remove all struggles and alleviate every roadblock. What He does do is build bridges that will carry us to joy, hope, and ultimately to heaven. The truth is, few of us comprehend the cost and sacrifice God has paid to build bridges for us to cross.

"*Trust is the bridge from yesterday to tomorrow, built with planks of thanks.*"

Talk About It

Tell about a marvel of human ingenuity (a bridge, building, modern-day technology, or something else) that has amazed you. What do you learn about the human capability for creativity and innovation when you look at this object?

Video Notes

As you watch the video for session four, use the following outline to record anything that stands out to you.

Praying for courage

A difficult journey of trust

Trust is hard work

What is true belief?

Practical atheism

Remembering and recounting

The bridge and the Bridge Builder

God ... fear conqueror

*"It's only when you live the prayer of thanksgiving
that you live the power of trusting God."*

Video Discussion and Bible Study

1. We all have things that can keep us from walking boldly through
   the doors God places before us. For Ann, agoraphobia and
   anxiety have been obstacles she has had to face. For others it can
   be depression, fear, a personal limitation, or something else. What
   is one roadblock you have faced as you seek to walk through the
   doors God has placed in front of you?

How has God helped you get past some of the roadblocks you have faced in your journey of faith?

"Thanksgiving is the one thing God asks to be done in everything and always.... He knows what precedes the miracle."

2. Ann tells of four dark and painful moments on her journey of life and faith, each of which made it hard for her to live with deep trust in God. Why is it critical for us to remember and acknowledge these times of pain and fear? What happens when we ignore or deny they exist?

3. In the video, Ann says, "Trust is work. Hard work." Do you agree or disagree with this? Describe how trust is hard for you, or easy for you.

"When we can't see His hand, we can always see His heart."

4. In the video, Ann says, "Jesus says that trust is our primary task: that we believe in the name of the One whom God has sent. That we have faith in His Messenger ... our Savior. That we trust the One who comes to save us." Where are you in this journey of learning to place your trust in Jesus as the one bridge to carry you over the fears, pains, and brokenness of this life?

What steps are you taking to grow more in this relationship with the Savior?

"*All* gratitude is ultimately gratitude for Christ,
all remembering a remembrance of Him."

5. **Read:** Psalm 40:1−5. Some people are able to trust in God only when things are going well. What do we learn from David's example of trust in Psalm 40? How does he view God and how does he look at his own life situation?

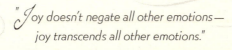

"*Joy* doesn't negate all other emotions—
joy transcends all other emotions."

6. **Read:** James 2:19 and Mark 16:15–16. Biblical belief is more than just giving mental assent to something. How do these two passages clarify the importance of a deeper belief that transforms our lives and leads to putting our faith and trust in Jesus?

   If you are a follower of Jesus, tell about when you first went beyond simple belief (mental assent) to placing your full trust in Him. If you are not yet a follower of Jesus, talk about what is holding you back from placing your full trust in Him.

7. Respond to this statement: "When we refuse to trust God and forget to live with *eucharisteo* thankfulness, we are living as practical atheists. We are not positional atheists (in truth, we are always positioned in Christ through faith in Him), but we are living like God does not exist."

8. Tell about a time when you faced a tough situation, but walked through it with deep trust and confidence in God. How did you experience God being with you as a bridge over the tumultuous waters below? How was joy unleashed?

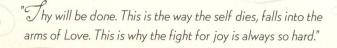

"*Thy* will be done. This is the way the self dies, falls into the arms of Love. This is why the fight for joy is always so hard."

9. In the video, Ann tells about a snowy day when she had an epiphany. On Road 178, at the edge of a bridge, it hit her. The Bridge Builder is trustworthy. We need to give thanks for the countless gifts He gives. There can be rough waters below. But God, the ultimate Bridge Builder, can be trusted! Share a moment in your life when you realized, deep in your heart, that God is trustworthy.

10. **Read:** James 1:2–4, Philippians 4:4–7, and Romans 15:13. What is the connection between trust and joy? How can trust in God become a bridge to lasting and growing joy in our lives?

    What are steps you can take in the coming week to trust God more so that you can walk in His joy?

Closing Prayer

Spend time in your group praying in any of the following directions:

- Invite God to help you identify and accept the hard times of life that we all face.
- Pray for growing levels of trust in God, no matter what you face.
- Ask for the Holy Spirit to grow joy in you as you learn to trust God.

- Declare your belief in God's goodness and the saving power of Jesus Christ.
- Ask God to help you remember His goodness in the past so that your trust grows and your joy overflows.
- Thank God that He is trustworthy, even in the hard times of life.

"*Is* it only when our lives are emptied that we're surprised by how truly full our lives were?"

⁓ between sessions ⌒

My Gifts

Use the space below or your own journal to list ten more gifts of grace.

-
-
-
-
-
-
-
-
-

Trust-Stretching Moments

In the video, Ann is honest and graphic about some of her trust-stretching moments: the loss of her sister Aimee, an ulcer at age seven, teenage turmoil, and the onset of panic attacks in her college years.

There is something helpful and healing about looking at the tough stretches of our journeys. Admitting that these moments exist and that we struggle with trust during these moments can actually drive us to find the bridges God has provided to help us make our way to His joy.

Trust–Stretching Moments

Write some personal reflections of a few trust-stretching moments you have faced along the road of your life.

Planks in the Bridge

Write down some of the "planks of trust" you can think of. In other words, identify ways God has been your Bridge Builder and the things He has done to show you He is present, powerful, and building bridges for you.

Noticing God's Activity Through My Week

Take time this week to notice ways God is bringing gifts into your life and write these new planks across the picture of the bridge below. Reflect on these as you celebrate the reality that God is still adding planks to your bridge each day.

Meditating on the Life-Changing Truth of God's Word

Write the words of Romans 8:32 across the picture of the bridge below. Reflect on the cost the Father and the Son paid to build the ultimate bridge for you.

Putting It in Your Own Words

Write a prayer across the bridge below, thanking God the Father for His sacrifice in sending His Son to bear your sins and become the Bridge for your salvation.

One of My Trust-Stretching Moments

How old was I? _____

What happened?

How this experience impacted my ability to trust God

A bridge God built to help me cross over to joy

My prayer for God to continue building a bridge of trust that will lead to joy

Another Trust-Stretching Moment
How old was I? _____
    What happened?

How this experience impacted my ability to trust God

A bridge God built to help me cross over to joy

My prayer for God to continue building a bridge of trust that will lead to joy

A Third Trust-Stretching Moment

How old was I? _____

　What happened?

　How this experience impacted my ability to trust God

　A bridge God built to help me cross over to joy

　My prayer for God to continue building a bridge of trust that will
lead to joy

"*Thanks is what builds trust.*"

Trust-Building Moments

Through the history of each of our lives are moments when we see the face of God, feel His touch, and know that He really is good and on the throne. It is vital that we remember these moments, recite them, and even talk about them with others.

Recount a few trust-building moments from the journey of your life.

One of My Trust-Building Moments

How old was I? _____

What happened?

How this experience grew my ability to trust God

My prayer of thanks to God for being a bridge-building and trustworthy God

Another Trust-Building Moment

How old was I? _____

What happened?

How this experience grew my ability to trust God

My prayer of thanks to God for being a bridge-building and trustworthy God

A Third Trust-Building Moment

How old was I? _____

What happened?

How this experience grew my ability to trust God

My prayer of thanks to God for being a bridge-building and trustworthy God

Pick one of these trust-building moments from your life and share it with a person who is younger than you. There is something glorious, beautiful, and powerful about recounting your story of God's trustworthiness. This process will strengthen your faith and theirs!

A Poetic Expression

The Southern writer Will Allen Dromgoole penned more than 7,500 poems in her lifetime, but none as well known or popular as "The Bridge Builder." In it she describes bridge building as not just what God does for each of us but what He then calls us to do for anyone else about to cross troubled waters.

The Bridge Builder

An old man, going a lone highway,
Came at the evening, cold and gray,
To chasm, vast and deep and wide,
Through which was flowing a sullen tide.
The old man crossed in the twilight dim;
The sullen stream had no fears for him;
But he turned when safe on the other side
And built a bridge to span the tide.

"Old man," said a fellow pilgrim near,
"You are wasting strength with building here;
Your journey will end with the ending day;
You never again must pass this way;
You have crossed the chasm, deep and wide—
Why build you the bridge at the eventide?"

The builder lifted his old gray head:
"Good friend, in the path I have come," he said,
"There followeth after me today
A youth whose feet must pass this way.
This chasm that has been naught to me
To that fair-haired youth may a pitfall be,
He, too, must cross in the twilight dim;
Good friend, I am building the bridge for him."

Will Allen Dromgoole (1860– 1934)

Who in your life is struggling to cross from one season to another, from one situation to another, whose trust in God is tentative? How might you practically be a bridge for that person today, this week—that he or she many know that God's love for them never ends?

"*Blessings never end because God's love for you never ends.*"

Journal

Use the space provided to reflect on any of the following topics:

- How God has used hard times to grow your trust in Him.
- Ways that you have experienced lasting joy as you have learned to trust in Jesus.
- Passages from the Bible that teach you of God's faithfulness and trustworthiness.

- Reasons you believe in God and can trust Him, no matter what you experience in this life.
- Bridge moments when you had a fresh new awareness that God is a trustworthy Bridge Builder.
- Ways you can share stories of God's faithfulness with people in your life who still have not met the Great Bridge Builder and Savior of your soul (including prayers for them to place saving and life-changing trust in Jesus).

Recommended Reading

As you reflect on what you have learned in this session, you may want to reread chapters 8–9 of the book, *One Thousand Gifts* by Ann Voskamp. In preparation for session five, you might want to read chapters 10–11.

SESSION 5

empty to fill

Introduction

The flow of the water, it begins from on high.

From high over the Mediterranean Sea, water vapor collects over the waves — and a cloud, the size of a man's hand, drifts in toward land. Those collected water vapors drift closer and rise higher to fall as snow on the 10,000-foot heights of Mount Hermon.

And then it flows.

The water flows into a river, the Jordan River, and flows downward into two other bodies of water — the Sea of Galilee and the Dead Sea.

The first to be fed from the freshwater of the Jordan is the Sea of Galilee. It receives water in the north and it gives from the south as the Jordan continues to flow downward. The Sea of Galilee, it teems with life; it is fresh, and alive with fish. If you dive into this clear water, you can open your eyes and swim freely.

The second body of water is the Dead Sea. It also receives from the north as the Jordan pours forth its freshwater. The difference is that the Dead Sea does not give. The Dead Sea just takes. There is no outlet! As a consequence, nothing can live in its toxic, mineral-filled, bitter waters. If you dive into this body of water and open your eyes, you will need to call a medic. It burns like acid!

Two seas fed by the same river. One gives and lives. The other holds on and dies.

What is true for these ancient bodies of water is just as true in our lives. When we receive gifts, grace, and joy, and give them to others, we are fresh and filled with life. And when we receive, take, and hold on to the good gifts of God and never pour out for others, we become bitter and toxic.

There is a water cycle of grace — His gifts fall from on high and are meant to flow on — and when we give the gifts away, the earth and His angels cry glory. The earth seems something of Christ in this giving away. And when we awake to how God is filling us—and then empty ourselves for others—we ourselves become more like Christ. We become like Him in His giving. And we begin to know the wild, uncontainable joy He knows in that giving.

But if we only receive His grace and never pour out of His grace? Something inside of us dies.

Joy dies.

And there are times it's too late for a medic. Why hold on—when you could let go and give and live?

"*Grace is alive, living waters.*"

Talk About It

Tell about a person you know who loves to give, serve, and share what he or she has with others. What kind of attitudes and character mark the life of this person?

"*A life contemplating the blessings of Christ becomes a life acting the love of Christ.*"

Video Notes

As you watch the video for session five, use the following outline to record anything that stands out to you.

An invitation to serve ... to take a chance

An encounter on Yonge Street

The only carpenter who can repair our world

Romans 7: A lesson from God and a man on the street

I can be the gift

John 13: Receiving gifts and giving gifts

Communion service and communion as service

Never stop counting your gifts

Video Discussion and Bible Study

1. Ann talks about a profound truth she learned from a very surprising source ... a broken man living on the edges of society. Tell about a time you heard someone speak something that struck you as profoundly true. What did the person say and what did you learn?

2. We live in a time when "regifting"—taking a gift you have received and passing it on to someone else—is quite common. But what if, as believers, we didn't regift what we no longer liked or wanted, but instead gave away our best, as God gave us His best? What are some examples of gifts God gives to you that you can regift and pass on to others? What would it mean if your week, your life became about this: "I am blessed. I can bless. So this is happiness!"?

3. **Read:** Romans 7:14–25. How does the apostle Paul's struggle and honest admission of his battle with sin resonate with your own life experience?

"When Christ is at the center, when dishes, laundry, and work is my song of praise to Him, joy rains."

4. When we serve with our focus strongly and solely on Jesus, our attitude stays healthy and our hearts continue to be joyful. List other possible consequences of serving out of love for Jesus.

   What are some dangers and potential pitfalls of offering acts of service with the intention of making people happy, getting something in return, or making people the focal point of our service?

   "When the eyes of the heart focus on God, all work becomes worship, a liturgy of thankfulness."

5. Select *one* of the following acts of service and describe how our hearts beat differently and our attitudes are healthier if we serve out of love and devotion for Jesus and not for the person we are serving:

   - Going on an international mission trip
   - Serving meals at a city mission
   - Holding worship services at a retirement center
   - Tutoring a child through a local school
   - Sponsoring a child through Compassion International
   - Buying a stranger lunch
   - Some other act of service . . .

6. **Read:** John 13:1 – 17. What do you learn about the heart of Jesus through this account?

7. This amazing act of foot washing happened at the same table where Jesus and His disciples celebrated the Last Supper. What significance do you see between communion (Jesus giving the bread and cup as a reminder of His body broken and blood poured out) and Jesus washing His followers' feet and calling them to do the same for others?

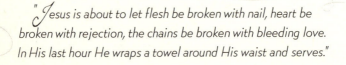

"*Jesus is about to let flesh be broken with nail, heart be broken with rejection, the chains be broken with bleeding love. In His last hour He wraps a towel around His waist and serves.*"

8. What are examples of simple and daily acts of service we can offer to God as we serve family, friends, and neighbors? What can stand in the way of us extending these acts of grace?

9. **Read:** Mark 10:45 and Luke 12:35–38. Describe a time when you were profoundly aware that Jesus was at work serving you.

How did this make you feel and how did it impact your desire to serve others?

"It is an astonishing truth that while I serve Christ, it is He who serves me."

10. What is an act of service you know God wants you to extend to someone in your life, but you have simply not gotten around to it? How can your group members encourage you, cheer you on, and keep you accountable to take this action in the name of Jesus? (Consider writing "I am blessed! I can bless! So this is happiness!" on an index card and taping it on the fridge, a mirror, or somewhere you'll be sure to read it frequently in the coming week.)

"Eucharisteo has taught me to trust that there is always enough God."

Closing Prayer

Spend time in your group praying in any of the following directions:

- Ask God to help you pour out His goodness and gifts as you receive them.
- Pray that you will have courage to remove your masks and let God and others see who you really are.
- Ask for God to make your church a place where people can be honest and transparent about their struggles and frailties and know they will still be loved.
- Invite God to use your hands to wash the feet of the people He places in your life.
- Pray that you will be like the Sea of Galilee and not the Dead Sea. May God's gifts and grace flow into and through you.
- Thank God for His gifts—and ask Him to show you how you can become the gift.

in the coming days

My Gifts

Use the space below or your own journal to list ten more gifts of grace.

-
-
-
-
-
-
-
-
-
-

"The one thousand presents wake me to the presence of God."

New Adventures

Ann knew the call of God to take on the challenge to go back to the same streets of Toronto where she had her first panic attack. This would not be a return to school, but a willing choice to go to a place of deep needs, profound suffering, and possible panic-inducing encounters. In her willingness to go, God wrote another chapter in her journey of *eucharisteo*. She got to live the wonder of "I am blessed! I can bless! So this is happiness!"

Think about and then write down three or four things you could do that would stretch your faith and cause you to trust God on a deeper level. Three or four things you could do to become the gift, that your thanksgiving might become thanks-LIVING. Things you could do in an afternoon, evening, or on a Saturday. Be bold, but realistic—a gift back to the Lord.

Possible adventure #1

Possible adventure #2

Possible adventure #3

Possible adventure #4

Pray about making a commitment to embark on a new adventure for God in the coming weeks or month. Seek wisdom in prayer, from wise believers, and from the Bible. Then, if you feel led to take a faith-growing, trust-increasing adventure, to make your life a gift— go for it! As you do, add to your list of gifts that God shows you along the way. It is always infinitely better to give than to receive!

Rivet It to Your Heart

To become God's gift receivers and gift givers, we need the simple yet powerful truths of His Word riveted to our hearts and engrafted to our souls. Take time to commit one or more of the following passages to memory and make it a part of your daily thinking and living:

> *For even the Son of Man did not come to be served, but to serve,*
> *and to give his life as a ransom for many. (Mark 10:45)*

> *Now that I, your Lord and Teacher, have washed your feet,*
> *you also should wash one another's feet. (John 13:14)*

> *Thanks be to God, who delivers me through Jesus Christ our Lord!*
> *(Romans 7:25)*

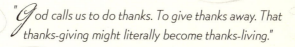

"*God calls us to do thanks. To give thanks away. That thanks-giving might literally become thanks-living.*"

Journal

Use the space provided to reflect on any of the following topics:

- Some of the ways you have missed opportunities to let God's good grace and gifts flow through you. Write words of confession as well as commitments to repent and turn in a new direction.
- How you have learned from people you would never have expected. What lessons have you learned and how have they impacted your life?

- Confession of the things that you want to do, but fail to do. Confession of the things you know you should not do, but you find yourself doing anyway. Prayer for power to live with greater obedience to the leading of the Holy Spirit in these areas of your life.
- Practical ways you can wash the feet of others and extend humble service in the name of Jesus.
- How you can open your hand to receive God's heavenly manna and keep your hands open to share the manna with others.

Recommended Reading

As you reflect on what you have learned in this session, you may want to reread chapters 10–11 of the book, *One Thousand Gifts* by Ann Voskamp.

small group leader helps

To ensure a successful small group experience, read the following information before beginning.

Group Preparation

Whether your small group has been meeting together for years or is gathering for the first time, be sure to designate a consistent time and place to work through the five sessions. Once you establish the when and where of your times together, select a facilitator who will keep discussions on track and an eye on the clock. If you choose to rotate this responsibility, assign the five sessions to their respective facilitators up front, so that group members can prepare their thoughts and questions prior to the session they are responsible for leading. Follow the same assignment procedure should your group want to serve any snacks or beverages.

A Note to Facilitators

As facilitator, you are responsible for honoring the agreed-upon time frame of each meeting, for prompting helpful discussion among your group, and for keeping the dialogue equitable by drawing out quieter members and helping more talkative members to remember that others' insights are valued in your group.

You might find it helpful to preview each session's video teaching segment and then scan the "Video Discussion and Bible Study" questions that pertain to it, highlighting various questions that you want to be sure to cover during your group's meeting. Ask God in advance of your time together to guide your group's discussion, and then be sensitive to the direction He wishes to lead.

Urge group members to bring their study guide, pen, and a Bible to every gathering. Encourage them to consider buying a copy of the *One Thousand Gifts* book by Ann Voskamp to supplement this study.

Session Format

Each session of the study guide includes the following group components:

- **"Introduction"** — an entrée to the session's topic, which may be read by a volunteer or summarized by the facilitator
- **"Talk About It"** — an icebreaker question that relates to the session topic and invites input from every group member
- **"Video Teaching Notes"** — an outline of the session's video teaching (about 20 minutes each) for group members to follow along and take notes if they wish
- **"Video Discussion and Bible Study"** — video-related and Bible exploration questions that reinforce the session content and elicit personal input from every group member
- **"Closing Prayer"** — several prayer cues to guide group members in closing prayer

Additionally, each session features a **"Between Sessions"** section with suggestions for personal response (including starting one's own list of God's gifts of grace), recommended reading from the *One Thousand Gifts* book, and journal prompts. Ideally, group members will spread these activities over several sittings rather than attempt to do them all at once.

One Thousand Gifts

A Dare to Live Fully Right Where You Are

Ann Voskamp

Just like you, Ann Voskamp hungers to live her one life well. Forget the bucket lists that have us escaping our everyday lives for exotic experiences. "How," Ann wondered, "do we find joy in the midst of deadlines, debt, drama, and daily duties? What does the Christ-life really look like when your days are gritty, long—and sometimes even dark? How is God even here?"

In *One Thousand Gifts*, Ann invites you to embrace everyday blessings and embark on the transformative spiritual discipline of chronicling God's gifts. It's only in this expressing of gratitude for the life we already have, we discover the life we've always wanted ... a life we can take, give thanks for, and break for others. We come to feel and know the impossible right down in our bones: we are wildly loved—by God.

Let Ann's beautiful, heart-aching stories of the everyday give you a way of seeing that opens your eyes to ordinary amazing grace, a way of being present to God that makes you deeply happy, and a way of living that is finally fully alive.

Come live the best dare of all!